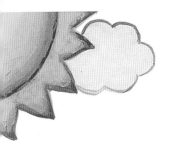

MW01223805

To: ....

who was baptized on: ....

at: ....

by: ....

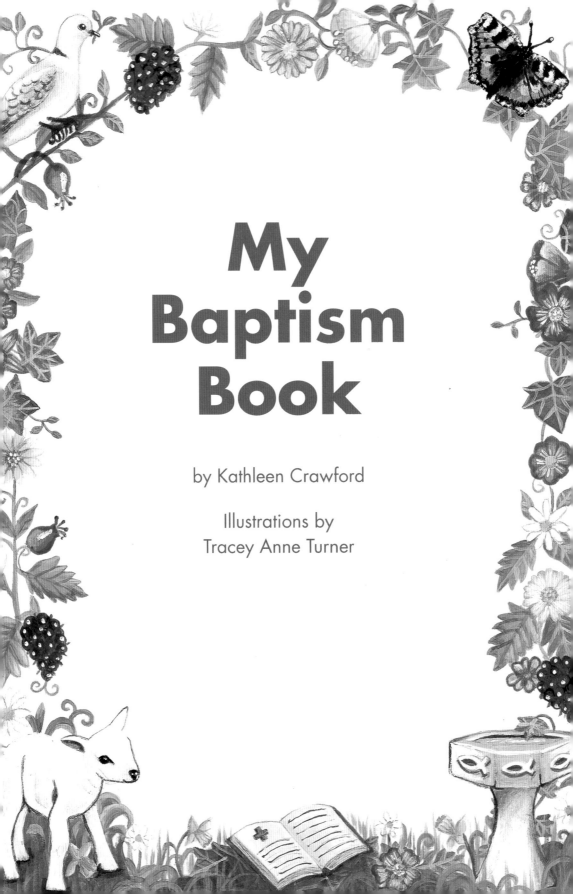

My Baptism Book

by Kathleen Crawford

Illustrations by
Tracey Anne Turner

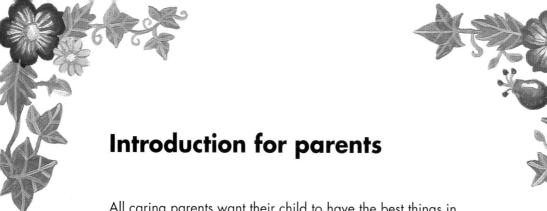

Introduction for parents

All caring parents want their child to have the best things in life – good health, security, and most of all, love. They realize that for their baby to grow into a well-adjusted adult they need to provide for his or her emotional needs as well as the physical ones. Every child needs to feel wanted, accepted and valued.

Many parents also want to provide for a child's spiritual needs. They want their baby to receive God's blessing and to grow up with a strong faith which will help him or her to cope even when life is difficult. And so they ask for baptism for their child – an occasion when they can thank God for the safe arrival of the newest member of their family, celebrate and, more importantly, see their baby welcomed as a member of the worldwide family of the Christian Church.

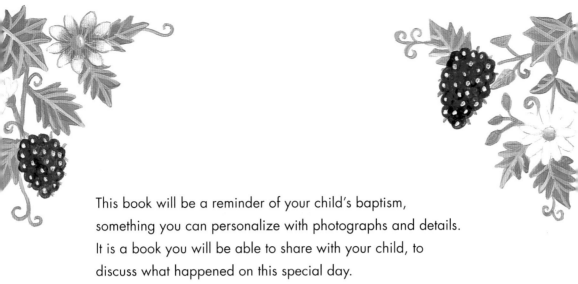

This book will be a reminder of your child's baptism, something you can personalize with photographs and details. It is a book you will be able to share with your child, to discuss what happened on this special day.

Using puzzles, pictures and fun activities, it provides ways of exploring the main themes and symbols of the Baptism service. It contains prayers you might like to use as your child grows older, and it will remind you and the godparents of the promises you made to help your child grow up in the Christian faith.

We hope you will find the ideas valuable as you and your child begin to discover together the meaning of baptism.

Your special days

The first special day in your life was the day you were born.
Your family were so happy that you had arrived safely. You
were very precious to them and they began to do everything
they could to love and care for you. You won't remember this,
but lots of people wanted to see you, cuddle you and
welcome you into the world.

Your second special day was when your family took you to
church to be baptized. During the service the minister made
the sign of the cross on your forehead and sprinkled you with
water. That was to show how very much God loves you too.
It was a very happy service and everybody wanted to
welcome you into God's family, the Church.

**This is a photograph of me
on my special day**

The cross

If you look around you, especially when you go to church, you will be able to see lots of crosses. Some are made of metal and some of wood or stone. If you go to church on the Sunday before Easter, Palm Sunday, you may be given a cross made from a palm leaf.

Sometimes people wear jewellery that is made in the shape of a cross, perhaps a necklace, earrings, or a badge on their jacket. Often it means that the person believes in Jesus.

The cross is a symbol that reminds us that Jesus Christ died on Good Friday and came alive again on Easter Sunday.

See how many different kinds of crosses you can find.

When the minister made the sign of the cross on your forehead, he or she said these words:

Christ claims you for his own.
Receive the sign of his cross.
Do not be ashamed to confess the faith of
Christ crucified.
Fight valiantly as a disciple of Christ
against sin, the world and the devil,
and remain faithful to Christ to the end of
your life.

It is not easy always to be kind and helpful and to do good things. Sometimes we do things we know are wrong. But Jesus forgives us and promises that he will go on loving us and helping us to do things which are right.

Belonging

Can you see which babies belong to which mother?

Animal babies usually look very much like their parents. They grow up to walk, swim or fly like their parents. They eat the same kind of food and live in the same kind of home. Human babies, too, often look like other members of their family. Sometimes they grow up to enjoy or be good at doing the same things like music, games, dancing or riding a bicycle.

Have a look at some photographs of members of your family when they were children. Find out which have the same colour hair, eyes or skin as you do. What activities do you enjoy doing together?

People often wear a badge or a uniform to show that they belong to a club, do a particular job, or go to a certain school. Do you recognize any of the badges or uniforms on this page?

Which ones show that people belong to God's family, the Church?

When we are baptized, we are accepted as new members of God's family. God wants us to enjoy learning more about him through going to church and spending time with other people who love him. He wants us to enjoy worshipping him as we pray and sing together. God is our heavenly Father who wants everyone in his family to be kind and loving, just like he is.

Water

Water is used as the main symbol at a Baptism service. In fact, a baptism cannot take place without it. The water itself has no special properties, but is used as a picture of the way God pours his love into our lives - cleansing us from the things that are wrong and giving us forgiveness and a new start. Water is a powerful force and has its dangerous side, causing destruction such as flooding. In the early Church, baptism was by immersion and also had the symbolism for all to see of a person dying to their old life and rising to a new life in Jesus Christ (Romans 6:3-4). In some countries and churches this is still the preferred method of baptism. In most churches, however, baptism is administered by pouring water on the person to be baptized, in the name of the Father, Son and Holy Spirit.

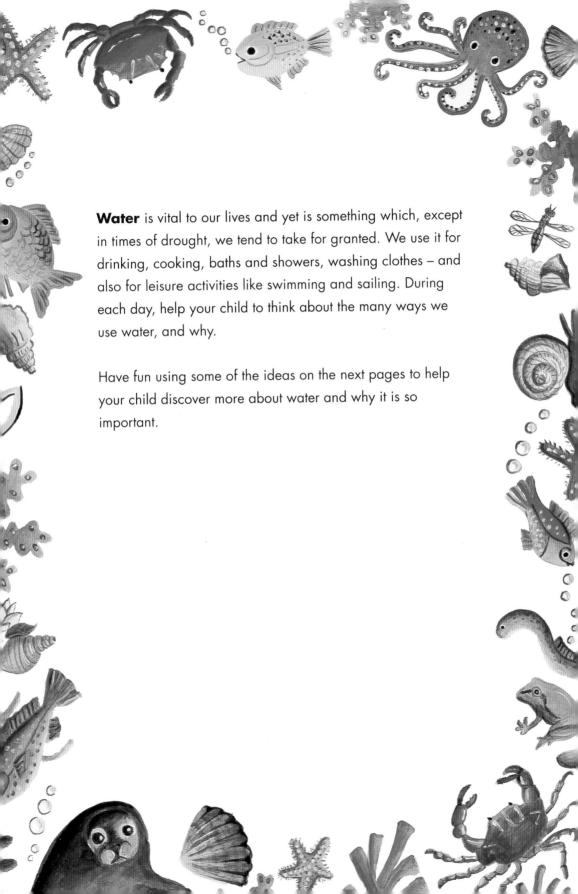

Water is vital to our lives and yet is something which, except in times of drought, we tend to take for granted. We use it for drinking, cooking, baths and showers, washing clothes – and also for leisure activities like swimming and sailing. During each day, help your child to think about the many ways we use water, and why.

Have fun using some of the ideas on the next pages to help your child discover more about water and why it is so important.

Water is very important. Without water, people, plants and animals would die.

Water is used in the Baptism service to show everybody how God wants to wash the wrong things out of their lives and give them a new, clean life instead.

We all use lots of water every day. We use it for washing, drinking, cooking food, having baths and showers, cleaning things, watering plants and having fun.

What happens if you put these things in water?

Bubble bath   Bath toys

Soap   Toothbrush

A sponge   Ice cubes

Which of the animals on this page live in water?

What would happen to them if there was no water?

What else can you see that badly needs some water?

This is the *Prayer over the Water* that was used at your baptism:

We thank you, almighty God, for the gift
   of water
to sustain, refresh and cleanse all life.
Over water the Holy Spirit moved in the
   beginning of creation.
Through water you led the children of Israel
from slavery in Egypt to freedom in the
   promised land.
In water your Son Jesus received the baptism
   of John
and was anointed by the Holy Spirit as
   the Messiah, the Christ,
to lead us from the death of sin to newness of life.

We thank you, Father, for the water of baptism.
In it we are buried with Christ in his death.
By it we share in his resurrection.
Through it we are reborn by the Holy Spirit.

Therefore, in joyful obedience to your Son,
we baptize into his fellowship those who come
   to him in faith.

Now sanctify this water that, by the power of
   your Holy Spirit,
they may be cleansed from sin and born again.
Renewed in your image, may they walk by the
   light of faith
and continue for ever in the risen life of Jesus
   Christ our Lord;
to whom with you and the Holy Spirit
be all honour and glory, now and for ever. Amen.

Light

In many churches candles are used during the Baptism service. They are a symbol of Jesus Christ coming into the world to bring light where there was spiritual darkness. They are also a reminder that Christians should continually reflect this light.

There are lots of ways you can explore the theme of light with children to help them build up a basic understanding of what light is and the effect it has.

Light helps us to see where we are going; it helps us to see clearly; it helps us not to be frightened of the dark; it helps plants and trees grow strong and healthy.

Candles are often used in celebrations because they make people feel happy.

A lighted candle may have been given to your family on behalf of your child. You might like to relight it on each anniversary of your child's baptism as a reminder of these words used in the Baptism service:

God has delivered us from the dominion
of darkness
and has given us a place with the saints in light.

You have received the light of Christ;
walk in this light all the days of your life.
Shine as a light in the world
to the glory of God the Father.

Light is important

When it is night-time, a light helps us to see where we are going. It keeps us safe from falling and hurting ourselves. It helps us not to be frightened. At sea, lighthouses warn ships that there are rocks nearby.

Light is important for plants and trees, too. It helps them to grow and be strong and healthy, with bright green leaves. Flower buds like the warmth of the sun and open up their petals to become beautiful flowers.

People feel especially happy if the sun is shining and they can feel its warmth.

On this page there are lots of different kinds of lights.

Which ones have you seen?

Which ones can you see in the sky?

Which ones help to keep you safe?

Which ones help you see clearly?

Which ones remind you of Christmas or parties?

Further ideas . . .

Sit in a room as it is getting dark. Light one candle and
watch for a few minutes how the flame flickers and glows
and begins to make a difference as it lights up the darkness.
Gradually light more candles, one at a time, so that the
effect of the light on the darkness is stronger. This is a
visual reminder that Jesus said we should shine as lights
in the world (Matthew 5:14-16).

Go as a family to a Christingle or candlelit carol service.
Experience the sense of light in the darkness.

On a clear night in winter, look at the stars and moon in
the sky. Notice the patterns of the twinkling stars and the
brightness of the moon against the dark sky.

On a day when the sun is shining brightly into a room, use a teaspoon, a shiny metal tray or a mirror to 'catch' the rays of sunlight and make them dance around the room. This can illustrate how Jesus wants us to reflect his love rather than keep it for ourselves.

On a sunny day, walk around the outside of a church or cathedral which has stained glass windows. Notice how the pictures may be seen but not clearly. Now go inside the building. Notice how the jewel bright colours of the glass are lit up by the sunlight. This is a picture of how it is easier to appreciate God's love for us when we are 'inside' his Church.

Welcome to God's family

When you were born you became part of a human family.

Your family are the people who look after you and love you.
Mums, dads, sisters, brothers, grandparents, aunts, uncles
and cousins are all part of your family, even if they do not
live in the same house as you do!

When you were baptized you became part of another family,
too. It is called the Church. Everyone who loves God is part
of his very big family – even if they live in a different part of
the world or have a different coloured skin from yours.

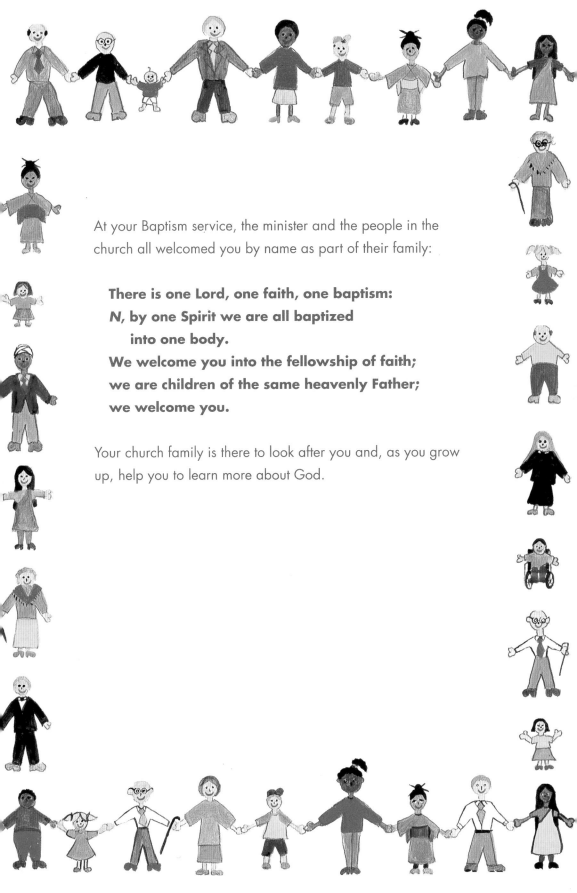

At your Baptism service, the minister and the people in the church all welcomed you by name as part of their family:

There is one Lord, one faith, one baptism:
_N_, by one Spirit we are all baptized
   into one body.
We welcome you into the fellowship of faith;
we are children of the same heavenly Father;
we welcome you.

Your church family is there to look after you and, as you grow up, help you to learn more about God.

Belonging to God's family

God loves us very much. He is like a good mother or father who wants to take care of us. He wants us to talk to him about the things that make us happy or sad, and the things that make us feel frightened. He wants us to enjoy discovering all the interesting things he has created.

God has promised that, wherever we are, he will be with us, and he will listen whenever we want to talk to him

Being baptized is just the beginning of getting to know God and understanding how much he loves each of us.

Some words from the Baptism service to remind you that
baptism is just the beginning of a relationship with God.

God has touched you with his love
and given you a place among his people.
God promises to be with you
in joy and sorrow,
to be your guide in life,
and to bring you safely to heaven.
In baptism God invites you on a life-long journey.
Together with all God's people
you must explore the way of Jesus
and grow in friendship with God,
in love for his people,
and in serving others.
With us you will listen to the word of God
and receive the gifts of God.

Godparents

Everybody who is baptized as a child has to have godparents. If you are a girl, you probably have two godmothers and a godfather. If you are a boy, you probably have two godfathers and a godmother.

Your godparents made promises for you in the Baptism service because you were not old enough to make them for yourself. At your Confirmation service you will be asked by the bishop to answer the same questions and make the same promises yourself.

Your godparents are people invited by your parents to pray for you and help you to learn about God. They have a special job to do in helping your parents to look after you.

My godparents are:

....

....

....

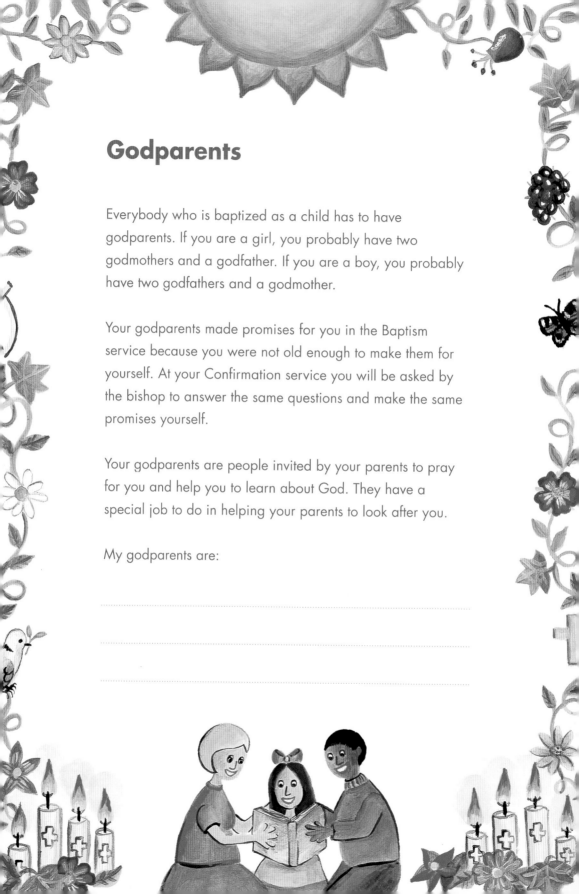

The minister said this special prayer for your parents and godparents. It asks God to help them to guide you and help you as you grow up.

Faithful and loving God,
bless those who care for this child
and grant them your gifts of love, wisdom
and faith.
Pour upon them your healing and reconciling love,
and protect their home from all evil.
Fill them with the light of your presence
and establish them in the joy of your kingdom,
through Jesus Christ, our Lord. Amen.

Prayers

Thank you that you love me

Sun shining brightly,
blue sky, wispy white clouds;
Strong wind is blowing,
grey sky, very black clouds;
Rain is pouring down,
miserable dark clouds.
Whatever the weather,
no matter how I'm feeling,
Thank you, God,
that you always love me.

Saying sorry

I didn't really mean it but somehow it just
    happened.
I didn't really mean it, when I made
    my friend sad.
I didn't mean to be unkind and I know
    you understand,
because Jesus you're the best friend
    that I've ever had.

Thank you, God, for water

Water for swimming, water for splashing;
Water to drink so cool and refreshing;
Water for paddling, cold water to squirt;
Water to wash in and get rid of the dirt;
Water in ponds where tadpoles grow;
Water in streams that down hillsides flow;
Water from rainclouds to moisten the seeds;
Thank you, God, for water to meet our needs.

The most famous prayer of all is called the Lord's Prayer. It is a prayer Jesus taught his disciples when they asked him if he would teach them how to pray.

Our Father in heaven,
hallowed be your name,
your kingdom come,
your will be done,
on earth as in heaven.
Give us today our daily bread.
Forgive us our sins
as we forgive those who sin against us.
Lead us not into temptation
but deliver us from evil.
For the kingdom, the power,
and the glory are yours
now and forever. Amen.

A prayer of thanksgiving

God our creator,
we thank you for the wonder of new life
and for the mystery of human love.
We give thanks for all whose support and skill
surround and sustain the beginning of life.
As Jesus knew love and discipline within a
    human family,
may this child grow in strength and wisdom.
As Mary knew the joys and pains of motherhood,
give these parents your sustaining grace and love;
through Jesus Christ our Lord. Amen.

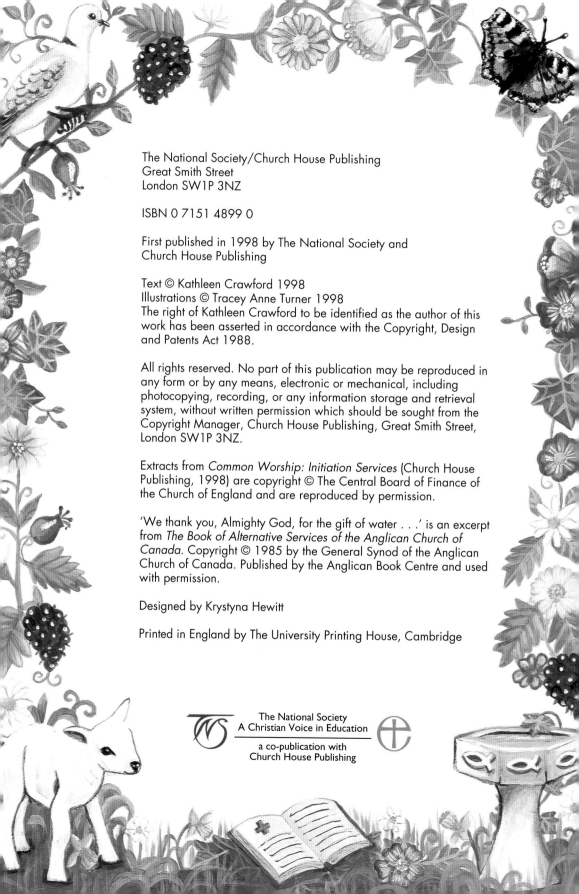

The National Society/Church House Publishing
Great Smith Street
London SW1P 3NZ

ISBN 0 7151 4899 0

First published in 1998 by The National Society and
Church House Publishing

Text © Kathleen Crawford 1998
Illustrations © Tracey Anne Turner 1998

Designed by Krystyna Hewitt

Printed in England by The University Printing House, Cambridge

The National Society
A Christian Voice in Education

a co-publication with
Church House Publishing